Ecclesiastical Reflections

Devotionals to help you ask yourself the tough **questions**

JEROME WRIGHT

KEVAN FERGUSON

ISBN: 9798609491442

An Introduction to

Ecclesiastical Reflections

Sometimes there are important unanswered questions in our lives. Some people are okay with these questions being unanswered and some are maybe not ok with them being answered. Either way it leaves us in a place of introspection to deal with some really not so nice issues.

There presently exists a healthy discourse about life issues in the media, on the job, at school, in our communities and our homes but seemingly we never really get to settle down long enough to answer all the questions about life and how to deal with the issues that press us day after day. Not only that but there are already so many answers to so many questions. For some the more we ask is the more questions pop up. All in all, it seems the issues are not that simple. Infact, they are very complex.

As God's word illuminates us and guides us to our next path, whenever we stop to look how far we have come from, we cannot but realize that it was His Word, His direction that brought us thus far and without his grace we would not have made it. Reflecting on life from a renewed spiritual standpoint, Solomon too realizes this as he catches wind of the fickleness of life amidst the challenges, triumphs and pitfalls he had made. A renewed Solomon terms himself as the preacher, after experiencing the treacheries of an idolatrous lifestyle, led on by a pagan wife, he sits himself down to think and ponder on his experiences. The sumtotal of his thoughts then have led to this book - Ecclesiastes.

Ecclesiastes is a hard-hitting, no bars holed kinda book. Many call it depressing but in fact it is full of life. It teaches us things learnt late in the game for Solomon and calls us to account for life's circumventing and neverending issues (without apology). With succinct language and clearness of speech, each verse charges us to face the facts and face them now.

This is your journey into those verses. I encourage you to read the recommended texts and answer the questions. Within these pages might just be the answers you have been looking for.

SOME PROFIT

"What **profit** hath a man of all his labor which he taketh under the sun?"

Ecclesiastes 1:3

Work can be tiresome and laborious. The hustle and bustle, the hum and drum, the go and come, the monotony of a routine and the quiet simplicity found in just being still can be lost in the midst of what some call our "daily grind". The simple goal of which most times is to provide for our most basic needs. The point of a job is to keep us busy yes but the point of work is to keep us in purpose. Looking back on the garden, Adam was not given labor only for labor's sake, but God created the garden for him to tend it. (see Gen2:15)

His work was connected to his purpose. I submit to you that today you may have lost sight of the real value of your labor and efforts but it is infact so that you may fulfill your God-given purpose. I hope that you like Jesus work with a constant recognition that your heavenly Father is also working, in purpose and on purpose on your behalf.

Recommended scripture: Mark 8
Question: Am I working in purpose or working in vain?

CONTINUAL CONTINUUM

"The wind goeth toward the south, and turneth about unto
the north; it whirleth about **continually**, and the wind
returneth again according to his circuits. All the rivers run
into the sea; yet the sea is not full; unto the place from
whence the rivers come, thither they return again"

Ecclesiastes 1:6-7

Live exists within a beautiful monotony. The arrangement of the
solar system, the mechanisms of biotic life and the flow of chemical
and mechanical energy to support living on Earth. Life is a beautiful
mystery. Human nature as well as the physical world we live in are
constantly enmeshed in a continuum that continues to go. It is
therefore important to understand that our lives are apart of this
continuum and that there befalleth us nothing that has not similarly
befallen those before us. We have history to use to our advantage and
the scriptures to use as a guide.

1 Corinthians 10:6 states:

> "Now these things were our examples, to the intent we
> should not lust after evil things, as they also lusted"

Let us therefore turn to the scriptures for guidance and search them
diligently to diagnose and remedy the same issues that befell our
ancestors. Prophesy to yourself today and say history will be kind to
me because I understand that history can be changed.

Recommended scripture: 1 Corinthians 10
Question: Am I willing to search the Scriptures for solutions or am I
content with non-biblical suggestions?

THE GOD GIVEN TASK (PART II)

"And I gave my heart to seek and search out by wisdom concerning all things that are done under heaven: this sore travail hath **God given** to the sons of men to be exercised therewith."

Ecclesiastes 1:13

The writer of the book of Ecclesiastes was a king over Israel. His observation that God gave a hard task was discovered after he keenly searched out the matter by discerning wisdom. His conclusion was God didn't give man an empty task.

Once I bought a 3-piece box of spicy chicken from KFC and I was so eager, I ripped open the box and started to devour the nice, crispy albeit greasy chicken. After I finished the meal, I noticed the writings on the box, "handbreaded" "flavored with 13 spices" and "storemade" and underneath it the caption " we don't make our chicken the easy way, we make our chicken the hard way"

I think that is what the God given task, the preacher was talking about, it is a task God has given to mankind to be exercised with, so that God we can be made stronger, not the easy way but the hard way.

Recommended Scripture: Matthew 11
Question: Does God always give us hard tasks?

GREAT EXPERIENCE

"I communed with mine own saying, Lo I am come to great estate, and have gotten more wisdom than all they that have been before me in Jerusalem: yea, my heart had **great experience** of wisdom and knowledge."

Ecclesiastes 1:16

Have you ever heard the saying experience teaches wisdom? I think that it is true because nothing teaches us more what we do not know than a good ole new experience. Experience is one of the best teachers. Theory is good, talking is good but when you are thrown into the ring of experience to see what it is like for yourself, I believe that is when you can really grow in wisdom. (see Luke2:40)

The Message version of this verse says that "I have stockpiled wisdom" In effect, I have collected and grown from the level of experiences. There is a value you must place on your experience in life because they have taught you and will continue to teach you wisdom.

Recommended Scripture: 1 Corinthians 2
Question: Have you learnt from your bad experiences as well as good ones?

I HAVE BEEN TO THE PARTY

I said to myself Lets go for it – experiment with pleasure,
have a good time! But there was nothing to it but smoke
Ecclesiastes 2:1 (MSG)

One author connoting the seasons of life penned that there are about eight seasons that a person will go through. He named the first three as the: *"drills, thrills and bills"*

These being representative of the ages: (0-15) (15-25) (25-45). The drills represent the age of being regimented, disciplined and socialized through school, the thrills represent the joys of ownership, a sense of freedom and autonomy from parental guidance and the bills represent the times of enormous financial obligation and restriction one has to undergo in later adulthood. The implication I want to share here is that the writer of Ecclesiastes was once in the drills perhaps as a young prince, soon after to gain the reigns of the throne. With a lifetime before him, he decided to enjoy the thrills, go to the parties, enjoy the "experiment" with pleasure and "live up" as we say. But at the end of it all he said, "it is all pointless."

If you were from a lifestyle that produced diminishing returns, would you not tell others that it is diminishing. This is coming from a guy with experience. He is telling us plainly been down that road, been there and done that and it is not worth it. He's been to the party and he knows what he is talking about.

Recommended Scripture: Matthew 22: 1-14
Question: Are you in the drills, thrills or bills of your life?

RIGHT REWARDS

"And whatsoever mine eyes desired I kept not from them, I withheld not my heart from any joy; for my heart rejoiced in all my labor: and this was my portion of all my labor."

Ecclesiastes 2:10

After a hard days work, you surely deserve some sleep and after a month long assignment at work you certainly deserve some pay. After you have cooked a meal, prepared the table, you certainly deserve to eat the meal. Well, the Ecclesiastical writer was saying he certainly deserved to have whatever he wanted. Maybe in his day he was the Burger King because he had to have it his way. (Did you laugh?)

Well Jokes aside. Labor deserves rewards and toil deserves recompense. Whenever we do something worthwhile, we should acknowledge that the reward is our portion. In the same breath, I want to remind you that doing right and laboring in righteousness rewards. The portion that you will receive will be worth it.

1Corinthians 15:58 says:

"Therefore, my beloved brethren, be ye steadfast, unmovable, always abounding in the work of the Lord, forasmuch as ye know that your labor is not in vain in the Lord."

Recommended Scripture: 1 Corinthians 15
Question: Did I do it my way or God's way?

DON'T INVENT THE WHEEL

And I turned myself to behold wisdom, and madness and folly: for what can the man do that cometh after the king? Even that which hath been already done.

Ecclesiastes 2:12

The wheel is an ancient invention. It is said to have been invented in Mesopotamia dating back to the BCE. It was a groundbreaking invention of its time as it revolutionized farming, transport and life as they knew it. Millenia later we are still using the wheel. Some of us use it everyday. Many of us cannot image life without the wheel today. It is staggering. Although the wheel of today is not the same as the one in Mesopotamia, the original invention has improved leaps and bounds due to advances in science and technology. In other words, old school wheels can thank new school wheels for the upgrade.

The wheel of change is still circular and sadly you can ask the preschooler, the circle will always be round. Change will always be change. In this passage the writer again points out the monotony of the circle of human existence – that what exists now in the human condition, will continue to exist, sure there might be some upgrades here and there but through and through – there really isn't anything completely new. It's a new thing from an old school.

Recommended Scripture: 2 Sammuel 23
Question: What area of my life is resistant to change?

NECESSARY EVIL?

For there is a man whose labor is in wisdom, and in knowledge, and in equity; yet to a man that hath not labored therein shall he leave it for his portion. This also is vanity and a great evil.

Ecclesiastes 2:21

The things that the Ecclesiastical writer calls evil amazes me. He mentions little about gross crimes and moral decadence but points to injustices and cyclical happenings as "grave evils". Come on! A man laboring and leaving it behind. That just sounds like life to me. But to him – not so. He calls it a great evil. Perhaps from his kingly perspective, after considering his own life and the lives of other great men who toiled, spent their lives laboring, fighting, legislating, doing bus strikes, being sent to jail.

Men like Nelson Mandela, Marcus Garvey, Martin Luther and Malcom X fought and labored in wisdom, fought for liberty and equity. But after their times there would have arose a generation that would have taken the liberties of no-segregated schools, no segregated water fountains and freedoms to sit anywhere on the bus for granted. Maybe just maybe from a kingly perspective, he might have considered the neglect and appreciativeness of those who they left behind as a great or necessary evil?

Recommended Scripture: Hebrews 11
Question: Am I laboring in wisdom, equity or love?

A GIFT FROM GOD

"I have decided that there's nothing better to do than go ahead and have a good time and get the most we can out of life. That's it- eat, drink and make the most of your job. It's God's gift."

Ecclesiastes 3:13

I like to speak in tongues. Sometimes I even run around the church. I like to see the gift of prophecy in operation and I have seen many testimonies as a result of the healing and deliverance ministry right before my eyes. I think it is very lovely and wonderful that God choses to work in such marvelous ways through imperfect pieces of clay. But guess what, those gifts from the Spirit, they are to edify the body of Christ. Sometimes, as in this instance, God gives no gifts that allow us to enjoy our everyday lives. Who would have thought a good hot meal, some time to relax, laugh and "galivant" (as we say in Jamaica) would be a gift from God. But it sure is. God is not endorsing gluttony here, but He is saying enjoyment of what he so graciously provides is apart of the package. Life, when its boiled down, to its bare components is: good, bad and ugly. Take some time to enjoy the good.

Recommended Scripture: 1 Corinthians 12
Question: When last have you reconnected to your God given gifts?

SET IN ETERNITY

"I know that, whatsoever God doeth it shall be forever: nothing can be put to it, nor anything taken from it: and God doeth it, that men should fear before him"

Ecclesiastes 3:14

Who said "forever ain't forever"? Maybe the guy who divorced you after saying the vows at the altar or the person who told you they are your BFF and the friendship fell through. I think we humans have a frail sense of the word 'forever' But God doesn't. He exists outside of time.

There are words that God has spoken in eternity that are still in motion today. (see Hebrews 1:3) He has separated himself from time and mingled with it for our benefit. Who are we to begin to understand what forever means? This verse shares with us a burst of revelation truth that when God puts his stamp on human activities, its eternally imprinted, and he does it so that men may reverence him.

Recommended Scripture: Hebrews 1
Question: Do I stand in awe of the majesty of God or do I treat him with paltry acknowledgement?

TIME LOOP

"That which hath been is now; and that which is to be hath already been; and God requireth that which is past"

Ecclesiastes 3:15

Time is an abstract and complex thing. God knows the end from the beginning. He is the Alpha and Omega. That means in the original language that he is not the beginning not the ending but he is the beginning in the ending. That puts a twist on it. Infact it lets me understand that in God's world, time is not on a linear progression but it is infact a loop of sorts, circular if you please. (For more information, I discussed it in my book, Laws of Spiritual Momentum)

When we begin to view time from God's perspective, we can see it not as fixed or rigid (as we may think from our human experience) but from his perspective it Is flexible. It is with this in mind that we see the writer penning a revelatory nugget encased in this verse. That which has been (the thing that has past) perceived to have happened already) is happening now, and that which is to be (the future) has already occurred. From God's heavenly perspective, one continual loop that he can adjust splice and edit for his glory. This is why the prophetic is so amazing, God through one prophetic word can change your past, present and future. The prophetic is like God's life and memory editing machinery. It can edit, enhance and embellish the movie-story of your life. For His Glory.

Recommended Scripture: 1 Sammuel 9
Question: Are there any bad patterns in my life that need editing?

THERE IS AN EVIL TIME

"I said to myself, God will judge righteous and wicked: There is a right time for everything, every deed and there's no getting around it. I said to myself regarding the human race, God's testing the lot of us, showing us up as nothing but animals."

Ecclesiastes 3:17

Amos 5:13 states: "Therefore the prudent shall keep silence in that time; for it is an evil time." As we sojourn through this Earth, we will experience times when God judges the righteous and times when he judges the wicked. God is a fair judge, as he judges what man does not see. These times for judgement are not set in stone but are by divine appointment. One must understand that there is a time for righteousness to abound and wickedness to be judged and another time for the prudent to be silent and the acts of wickedness to be shown up or revealed. The prophet Amos spoke of this time – he called it an evil time. Certainly, the lot of us have felt it, times when God tests the heart of man, exposes and judges their righteous and unrighteous deeds and shows them who they truly are.

Recommended Scripture: Amos 5
Question: Are you ensnared in an evil time?

TESTED TO BE MANIFESTED

> "I said in my heart regarding the subject of the sons of men,
> God is trying (separating and sifting) them that they may see
> that by themselves [under the sun without God] they are but
> like beasts"
>
> Ecclesiastes 3:18 (AMP)

What do you do when you failed to study for a test? Are you like me and cram minutes before the exam? Or do you just not go to the exam? I think God likes to test us and pull pop-quizzes all the time. These pop-quizzes are as the writer says to "try, separate and sift" the lot of us. In surety, God's testing comes with a purpose.

1Peter 4:12 says:

> "Beloved, think it not strange concerning the fiery trial which
> is to try you, as thou some strange thing happened unto you."

They are for our refinement. Oftentimes before precious metals undergo refinement, they do not look, smell or feel precious. They are often extracted from deep within the Earth (hidden and discovered through excavation). It is when it is sifted from the Earth and goes through the process that it is made fit for use. This what God does when he tests us, he manifests us to assess us for refinement.

I NEED A COMFORTER

"So I returned, and considered all the oppressions that are done under the sun: and behold the tears of such as were oppressed, and they had no comforter; and on the side of their oppressors there was power; but they had no comforter"

Ecclesiastes 4:1

Looking at the grim time of the Holocaust when Nazi soldiers slaughtered millions of Jews, strewn them in gas chambers, work them liked slaves. Oppression is a cruel taskmaster. We cannot begin to imagine the intense pain, torment and weakness the Jews endured at the hands of the tyrant oppressors, if they tried to escape or revolt, the Nazi's could and would mercilessly kill them. They were an oppressed people group and had no one physically fighting for them, no one but themselves who could lend support.

Oppression, tyranny, slavery and trafficking are social ills most of us today in the Western World are against but there exists another group who believe it is there right to oppress and disrespect human life. This group of oppressors are those that provoke the tears of the oppressed to cry for justice. These cries for justice almost always never go unheard by Heaven.

Oppression is a dark, spiritual force that gladly can be broken. The oppressor's power can be broken and the liberating power of God's Holy Spirit (the Comforter) can invade and uplift the bowed down oppressed to a place of dignity again. Are you in a place of spiritual or physical oppression? Cry out to God, he hears the righteous and saves such that be oppressed.

GRATITUDE IS A MUST

"Better is an handful with quietness, than both the hands full with travail and vexation of spirit."

Ecclesiastes 4:6

Being grateful for the least of blessings is a helpful practice to have. It lightens the mood of your day and helps you to keep focused on the good things in life. Koffe, a Jamaican artist wrote a song that caught me saying "Gratitude is a must" Funny enough a cup of Jamaican coffee is very expensive, a handful of the coffee beans is worth a lot, but infact the real value for me is in the coffee drink. People who can afford to buy Jamaican coffee should be grateful (I am saying this because I live in Jamaica and I cannot afford Blue Mountain coffee.) This is because I have learnt that what a handful of coffee beans is worth; can't buy a handful of peace. And what a cup of coffee can do cannot erase what peace of mind and the sweet sleep it brings can do. That's why whether you can buy Jamaican Blue Mountain coffee or not, Gratitude is a must.

Recommended Scripture: Psalm 111
Question: What are you most grateful for today?

POLITICAL LESSONS

"For out of prison he cometh to reign; whereas also he that is born in his kingdom becometh poor"

Ecclesiastes 4:14

Have you ever heard the name Nelson Mandela? He was one of the South African freedom fighters that went to jail for his stance against Apartheid, who after his acquittal became president. I am not sure if Solomon was prophesying about Mandela but one thing, we can learn from them both. Kings are not made in the palace; they are made in the prisons (confinement).

- Joseph was put in a prison and became ruler second in command.
- Daniel was put in the lion's den – a prison for lions.
- David was put in solitary confinement after being in exile from Saul.

There is something about confinement that teaches men to reign. It could be the severe treatment of learning how to submit and be led, or the rationing of resources to make due, it could be that you learn to read and lead your thoughts or you look forward to the day when you are establish your life's plans again. I am not entirely sure, but one thing I know men who have been in the trenches certainly are fit both to clean and to live in the castle, because they appreciate it and treat it for what it is.

Recommended Scripture: Joshua 5
Question: What are you taking for granted?

ONLY A FEW WORDS

"Be not rash with thy mouth, and let not thine heart be hasty to utter anything before god: for God is in heaven and thou upon the earth: therefore let thy words be few."

Ecclesiastes 5:2

Sometimes my favorite prayer to pray is "Help Lord" or "Mercy Jesus". In the daily throes of my routine, I sometimes just whisper it or shout it aloud. I have learnt to let my spirit always pray. (see 1Chorinthians 14:14) but more so these short bursts of prayer keep my memory fresh that talking to God is less about saying what you mean but more about meaning what you say.

Jesus said the Pharisees "Pray with much speaking" (Matthew 6:7) The fact is God doesn't need an explanation. He already knows what you want and need before you ask. (see Matthew 6:8) What he wants is heart to heart conversation and that transaction between heaven and earth is less about human words but more about Heaven's heart.

Recommended Scripture: Matthew 6
Question: After you pray, do you feel like you have connected with God?

OF A DIFFERENT KIND

For in the multitude of dreams and many words there are also divers vanities: but fear thou God.

Ecclesiastes 5:7

Somethings weigh heavily upon your spirit, while others don't. On a weekly to a monthly basis, the conversations we have, watch, interact with or over hear often feed into our subconscious mind without us even realizing it. Being so socially hardwired and connected lends us to begin to figure out how to navigate through our conversations on the phone, in person, reply to email, talks over lunch, dinner, on the way home, in the car, on the bus, or on the train. We simply get caught up in the flow of it all. In the midst of it, here comes the day dreams of our lives and the night dreams of our lives.

Our conversations and dreams that center around us and the many things we have to deal with immerse us into a sea of different and diverse vanities. If you don't stop in the midst of it all, take a break from the phone, the conversations about your dreams, goals and aspirations and spend time with God, very soon you will be swimming in a pool of stuff that you losing your focus and faith in God. Take some time to pause and reverence God's presence and make it a regular practice – everyday.

Recommended Scripture: Matthew 14:23-35
Question: Do I take time to focus on God or am I distracted by different vanities?

RACKETTERING

"If thou seest the oppression of the poor, and violent perverting of judgement and justice in a province, marvel not at the matter: for he that is higher than the highest regardeth; and there be higher than they."

Ecclesiastes 5:8

Racketeering can be defined as robbery, destruction of property or extortion related crimes. Sometimes the very system made to protect and defend us becomes the very system that disappoints and misconstrues us. This can certainly be alarming for those on the right side of the law. However, there is a system of accountability. There is nothing that occurs that people will not give account of for one day.

Romans 14:12 states:

> "So then everyone of us shall give account of himself to God."

A day will come when we will all have to pull up our life's statement of accounts and be expected to view the balance of our lives whether in negative or positive. By our own estimations, the accountability systems of man can fail us, but God's account system will never fail and that is good news for those on the right side of the law.

SUPPLY AND DEMAND

"When goods increase, they are increased that eat them: and what good is there to the owners thereof, saving the beholding of them with their eyes"

Ecclesiastes 5:11

Supply and demand is an economic concept which posits that when the supply of goods and there is no demand for them are high prices are low but when the supply of goods is low and there is a demand for them, it drives the price up. Business owners often use this seasonally and yearly to adjust their prices for best profits. Economically speaking, supply and demand is a law that governs pricing and buyer response. The spinoff affects many other areas of business.

Interestingly, before business intelligence tools where developed, the concept is found here in scripture. The Bible is laced with insights about business, science, governance, medicine, transport and artistry that predates and has also outlined the writers. Supply and demand is just one example. Is it possible that the preacher was also a shrewd businessman? We may not know it, but it is certainly a valid principle that when demand for a commodity is high, the stock will go quickly because it is in demand. That is to your benefit if you are the business owner, if not then you will be the one grasping for the bargain. I encourage you today to plug into the insights of the scripture not only to be a buyer but an owner.

HOW DID YOU COME? HOW WILL YOU GO

"There is a sore evil which I have seen under the sun, namely, riches kept for the owners thereof to their hurt. But those riches perish by evil travail: and he begetteth a son, and there is nothing in his hand. As he came forth of his mother's womb, naked shall he return to go as he came, and shall take nothing of his labor, which he may carry away in his hand. And this also is a sore evil, that in all points as he came, so shall he go: and what profit hath he that laboreth for the wind."

Ecclesiastes 6:16

One thing that always stands out about the Ecclesiastical writer is what he considers evil. Before we discussed what, he calls "great" evil but now he labels the passing of a working-class man with a son as a sore evil. The Amplified Version calls it a "serious and severe evil" The evil to be considered here is that as the man came in the Earth so did, he leave. In other words:

He came   He left
- Without money   - Without money
- With sin and its effects   - With sickness and sadness
- Without satisfaction in life   - Without satisfaction in life

This is certainly not a good thing to see. Our time on Earth was made to change something. This man perhaps did not know or have a personal relationship with God. That is perhaps why he came, he left. The good news is Jesus came, so you didn't have to go, how you come. You can be born, die and be born again through him.

Recommended Scripture: John 3

Question: Have you accepted Jesus as your personal Lord and Savior?

ANSWER OF THE HEART

> "Every man also to whom God hath given riches and wealth and hath given him power to eat thereof, and to take his portion and to rejoice in his labor; this is the gift of God. For he shall not much remember the days of his life; because God answereth him in the joy of his heart"
>
> Ecclesiastes 5:19-20

One year after attending a prophetic service, the speaker asked us to speak out loud what we wanted for Christmas, I asked God for a laptop for that Christmas. Some days after the service, within the same week, someone offered to buy me a laptop for Christmas. I rejoiced at the answer to prayer and thanked the Lord for my Christmas present.

Jesus said in John 16:24 that:

> "Hitherto have ye asked nothing in my name: ask and ye shall receive, that your joy may be full."

There is something about answered prayers that makes us happy. Better yet when it is fulfilled in its proper time, we can rejoice and remember the time stamp, the exact amount when we got what we were praying for. Sometimes God answers prayers our mouths are yet to pray, but that our hearts have prayed. These answers often come to person who God knows will be happy with what he gives. This maybe the way, the timestamps fade the memories away as joy causes the heart to delight because prayers the man have not prayed are being answered and the heart is fulfilled and excited knowing that God is answering it and filling it with joy. Just sheer joy!

Recommended Scripture: John 16

Question: Is your life marked with answered or unanswered prayers?

LOST POWER

"A man to whom God hath given riches, wealth, honor, so that he wanteth nothing for his soul of all that he desireth, yet God giveth him not power to eat thereof, but a stranger eateth it: this is vanity , and it is an evil disease"

Ecclesiastes 6:1-2

Is it possible for God to give you something and not give you the enablement to enjoy it? You must begin to consider the words of the scripture above, that with every blessing comes the enablement of the blessor. I have once heard it said that "When the praises come up, the blessor comes down." Many times, people get the blessing but forget the blessor. And this should not be so.

The God who blesses and gives us power to get wealth. (see Deut. 8:18) is the same God who can and will withhold the ability to enjoy it. Sometimes this might seem like a nuisance, but it is actually a blessing. The eyes that are trained can spot this that when gives something and withholds something and the power to enjoy it. It might be that God is teaching you that he alone is to be worshipped (not the creation but instead the creator.) Whenever we give or sacrifice time, effort, money or energy for any [material] or [human] endeavor more than we do for the things of God and of the kingdom of God we are being pulled into idolatry and that is a very risky place to be in. The Lord then in his love spares us from being lovers of vanity by allowing us to see that it is he that controls both the resource as he is the Source, he can give the goods to whomever he will.

Recommended Scripture: 1 Kings 14
Question: Have I lost power by giving into idolatry?

YOU HAVE TO SEE GOOD

"If a man beget an hundred children, and live many years, so that the days of his years be many, and his soul be not filled with good, and also he have no burial, I say that an untimely birth is better than he. For he cometh in with vanity, and departeth in darkness, and his name shall be covered with darkness. Moreover he hath not seen the sun, nor known anything: this hath more rest than the other. Yea though he live a thousand years twice told, yet hath he seen no good: do not all go to one place?"

Ecclesiastes 6:3-6

The allegory presented in this verse speaks of a man of many sexual relations, that had many children and lived a long life (perhaps on account of good health). Physically, he had a well to do life. But his soul had not seen any good. (v6) Didn't Jesus testify that a man's life consists not of the things he owneth. (see Luke 12:15) This man had lived a very long life, had health, had children, but was lonely, isolated and ignorant. This left him in a state of darkness. And what a darkness it was that covered his soul. Jesus said:

"Your eyes are the windows into your body. If you open your eyes wide in wonder and belief, your body fills up with light. If you live squint-eyed in greed and distrust, your body is dank cellar. If you pull the blinds on your windows, what a dark life you will have"

Matthew 6:22 (MSG)

It is often said that the eyes represent the windows to our soul.

Could it be that the man devoid of experiences of joy, seeing joy, seeing happiness, seeing hope fulfilled, seeing true prosperity had made his eye dim and eventually darkened? Could it be that the man although he lived long and had many children only saw murder, crime, hatred, malice, envy and it made him callous to life?

The simple fact is you are affected by what you see. Make it a priority to ensure that you see good things in your lifetime.

Recommended Scripture: Luke 7
Question: Do you expose yourself to good things consistently?

LUST AND CONTENTMENT

"Better is the sight of the eyes than the wandering of the desire: this is also vanity and vexation of spirit."

Ecclesiastes 6:9

There was a time in my life when all I wanted was icecream on a cone with smothering chocolate and yummy gummy bears. But as I grew up my taste became more sophisticated and I wanted a beautiful tub of smooth, flushing velvety icecream with infused fruits and nuts, just an holistic treat. Soon after I wanted icecream fudges in all shapes and forms. I was an icecream maniac. I just love icecream (sorry if your lactose)

But the truth is when the icecream was not being payed for by me, I could desire, ask and have it when I wanted it. But when I was the one paying, sometimes the stomach would be willing but the pocket would be weak. There would be no icecream that Sunday night. I had to be content without it.

Paul says to Timothy: "But godliness with contentment is great gain." (1 Timothy 6:6) We must understand that desire is a fruit of the appetite. Whatever we desire it must be born from our appetite and desire to be like Christ and to be content with being so. When you set your face before the Lord and behold the pleasures forevermore (from his presence) suddenly your appetite changes and even if you eat ice cream that Sunday night, you are simply content to be with him – in his presence.

24HRS TO GO

"It is better to go to the house of mourning than to go to the house of feasting: for that is the end of all men; and the living will lay it to his heart."

Ecclesiastes 7:2

What would happen if there were 24 hrs. left to be alive? What would be your resolve? Sometimes when faced with death, near death experience or the loss of a loved one we recognize what really matters. These occasions tend to bring us back to a semblance of what truly matters.

James 4:14 says:

"Whereas ye know not what shall be on the morrow. For what is your life? It is even a vapour, that appeareth for a little time, and then vanisheth away"

When we consider what life is and how truly frail and precious it is. Our response should be to lay it on your heart that life is a gift from God to us.

BROKEN HEARTS FIX BROKEN MINDS

"Sorrow is better than laughter: for by the sadness of the countenance the heart is made better"

Ecclesiastes 7:3

This past year I went to the US embassy in my country and was denied. I went in faith believing after hearing different prophetic voices in my parish speak declare visas and travelling. Sadly, I wasn't approved. I was upset at first then sad about it. I was hanging on to those words for a gleam of hope. But in my sorrow, I began to think and slowly realized that if I had gotten the visa, I would not have learnt the lessons I learnt. At the time I was not thinking through my decisions and acted in haste when I should have waited on the Lord to speak to me – for myself.

There is something about sorrow that causes the mind to think. It fixes something inside of our minds and causes us to restructure our thoughts for a better output of performance. Broken hearts can oftentimes be the steppingstone to fixing our broken minds. There is a lesson from the pain and recovery in the growth. Let it heal that you may grow.

TAKE THE REBUKE

"It is better to hear the rebuke of the wise than for a man to hear the song of fools"

Ecclesiastes 7:5

I am sure you have a favorite song that makes you go silly. For me it is not hallelujah but that song that goes mommy shark, daddy shark dup bup doo. It just a fun simple song. As much as these songs make light the mood. The true and stern correction of a person who has lived wisely is to be much more heard than these. If it had been so, many persons would be saved from many calamities. But as present this is not the reality. Persons often hate rebuke and despise those who correct them by snarling, retorting or begrudging but very often these are the same persons who ask for help.

However, they want help – on their own terms. There must be an appetite for wisdom in us and with that appetite often comes the callaloo, pok choy and string beans of rebuke that cleanse us out from the inside-out. It is my personal opinion for every credit or word of affirmation I deserve 5 rebukes. I personally do not want to hear too many good things about myself. I would rather hear about the good deed of others. Rebukes keep me sane and sober. How about you?

Recommended Scripture: Galatians 5
Question: Do you like or hate rebukes from teachers or mentors?

GIFTS

"Surely oppression maketh a wise man mad; and a gift destroyeth the heart."

Ecclesiastes 7:7

How can bad things make good things bad? And how can a good thing make something bad? It is an interesting paradox to observe. The Bible is filled with many such instances of paradoxes but this one baffles me more than others.

But I have found out by way of revelation that spiritual oppression lays men to be held by heavy yokes and spiritual gifts can cause the heart to be lifted up in pride. It takes the formation of sound character by the Holy Spirit to elevate above spiritual oppression and spiritual corruption.

Recommended Scripture: 1 Corinthians 14
Question: What do you think will happen if there is no character but much spiritual giftedness?

ANOTHER BUSINESS DAY

"Wisdom is good with an inheritance: and by it there is profit to them that see the sun. For wisdom is a defence, and money is a defence: but the excellency of knowledge is, that wisdom giveth life to them that have it"

Ecclesiastes 7:11-12

In math class, I learned that profit is a business term (not a spiritual one) – the spiritual one is prophet. It is calculated when the selling price allows the seller to make more money than they bought the raw materials for.

Solomon says here that having the ability to wisely manage one's good is beneficial, because by wisdom's shrewd management not only will you receive goods but add to them and in return gain a profit. The truth is when one gets wisdom, it increases business acumen and not only so it enhances your entire life. Who then wouldn't want some wisdom?

Recommended Scripture: Proverbs 1
Question: Do you have an appetite for wisdom?

FRACTIONS

"In the day of prosperity be joyful, but in the day of adversity consider: God also hath set the one over against the other, to the end that man should find nothing after him"

Ecclesiastes 7:14

Life is stacked. It comes with shelves and compartments that go higher and go higher. The older you get the more time you spend seeing and understanding, going through the rhythm and remembering that there are good days and bad days. A song I keep on singing of late called Be grateful has the line, a little rain a little pain so that you can appreciate the good times. I love that line "appreciate the good times"

Life in this way is not only stacked like a shelf but it is like a fraction. With a numerator and denominator. It has an overarching cause and an underlying cause. And just like a fraction it consists of a greater part and a lesser part. There are great days and not so great days. Days of joy and prosperity and days of adversity. Life is a varied experience and good will always stay atop evil. Life is like a fraction because God has set it so, one type of season over the other.

Recommended Scripture: Acts 13
Question: Are you in an adverse situation currently?

ACCOUNTING

Ecclesiastes 7:27

Once I was in a prayer meeting and I called a young man and said to him the Lord as you walk to count your steps. As he nervously did it, a few minutes later, I asked him what was he studying? He said accounting. This entire prayer meeting exclaimed in laugher. This is what you call a word of knowledge.

When I read this verse, I remembered this instance. I have seen this gift in operation several times stating facts about persons that are astounding. One such instance I encountered while I was on my school campus evangelizing during homecoming. I walked over to an expo where they had tents. I went up to a condom tent that sampled condoms and sex toys and began to speak to a young lady. She so happened to be the brand ambassador. As I introduced myself and spoke with her, as the conversation grew deeper, I had one of these word of knowledge promptings again and as I shared it with her she confirmed yes it was true. I had told her a detail about her family, a detail about her life and a reason she left the Christian faith, as the conversation opened up and reached the end. I quickly shared the gospel with her and told her about what the Lord would do for her if she returned to the faith. She remained resolute in her stance, but I believed she was called to account that day. So many people need to be reminded that God knows everything about them and that he indeed does reveal to redeem.

Recommended Scripture: John 4
Question: Have you ever had a word of knowledge?

WISDOM PILLS

"Wisdom strength the wise more than ten mighty men which are in the city."

Ecclesiastes 7:19

We all get tired. We can all get fatigued. None of us is immune to it. Even the best of us and the most driven sometimes need a boost of coffee or a pop of multivitamin to supplement our energy. But what do you do when your spirit is tired? Or your emotions are tired of a situation? What do you do when you are capable, able and qualified to handle a task, but you are too fatigued to do it? I hear you say Rest. Well that is when my friend, you do rest and allow wisdom to strengthen you. Like a shot of expresso or a iron pill supplement – wisdom can strengthen you. It can add to your mental, emotional and spiritual strength. No matter what state you are in, wisdom can help you and strengthen you there.

Recommended Scripture: Proverbs 4
Question: Do you add wisdom to your diet daily?

WORD POWER

"Where the word of a king is, there is power: and who may say unto him, What doest thou?"

Ecclesiastes 8:4

A person who possess royal office has be given authority. Today, we might see authority as only a person who has been given a right to act or permission but in the medieval era, authority was granted by sovereign right. If a person was not born in a family, he or she would not have the opportunity to even be considered as "authorized" or "having an important viewpoint."

Today by the democratic process and freedom of speech everyone has a say if they want to have a say in everyday matters. Time has changed the tides of who a say in what. However, time has not changed the tides of who has a say in what. However, time has not changed the fact that the voice of authority causes things to happen. When a person with authority (delegated power, right or permission) requests something it is done. Simply because of the office he holds. He/she has discriminatory influence. This is the power that authority provides. It gives us word power.

Recommended Scripture: Luke 10:17
Question: Do you use your authority given by God?

HEDGED

"Whoso keepeth the commandment shall feel no evil thing: and a wise man's heart discerneth both time and judgement"
Ecclesiastes 8:5

Obedience to God provides spiritual protection. Satan could not attack Job the way he did if God did remove the "hedge of protection" from around him. (see Job1:10) A hedge is a fence, protection or restraint. Spiritually, it is like a forcefield that repels negative influence from around you. Like a mosquito repellant if you please. This is what obedience in covenant relationship does it forms a force field around you, and you will feel no evil thing as a result because you are hedged about. Hallelujah.

Recommended Scripture: Job 1
Question: Are you hedged about?

YOUR MIGHT

Whatsoever thy hand findeth to do, do it with thy might; for there is no work, nor device, nor knowledge, nor wisdom, in the grave, wither thou goest.

Ecclesiastes 9:10

Meaningful work and employment is a blessing from God. While you are upon the Earth you should be productive and use your time wisely. This verse speaks of the might that God has given us to accomplish tasks with. The writer states it as your might. Therefore, it has a limit. It will end, it will run on empty one day. So, make sure whatever you do, you love it and do it well so that when your might runs out, it will be well spent.

Recommended Scripture: Matthew 20
Question: Are you wasting your time?

CAN A NET BE EVIL?

For man also knoweth not his time: as the fishes that are taken in an evil net, and as the birds that are caught in the snare, so are the sons of men snared in an evil time, when it falleth suddenly upon them.

Ecclesiastes 9:12

In a previous chapter, we spoke an evil time. But did you know the Bible talks about a evil net? I didn't until I read it. I didn't know a net could be evil. (Coincidently, my mother's name is Annet and I hope she doesn't read this chapter) I thought they were just nets, just a plain ole gizmo to be used by a fisherman. The writer is speaking an allegory which is a shadow of a spiritual truth. Spiritually, there are times that fall upon people that gather them and sweep them up – in effect displacing them. The net represents restriction and limitation. The mission of the evil net is to sweep up, displace and restrict but just as at the word of the Lord at the command of Jesus the net broke. Even so the evil net can be broken.

Recommended Scripture: Psalm 9
Question: What in your life needs to be broken?

VERANDA MEETINGS

The words of wise men are heard in quiet more than the cry of him that ruleth among fools

Ecclesiastes 9:17

There was a time in my life where I sat and met with a pastor and a small group once a week every week. The scriptural discussions, impartation, exchange and relationships I formed from that meeting are priceless. In that season of my life, I needed those meeting to keep me sober, keep me sane, keep me on the right track. The level of wisdom that was imparted impacted my daily walk so much that I longed for the meetings weekly. They were not loud, unobstructed and powerful – even life changing.

Instead of going to a party, spending 40, 00 JMD for VIP to hear a dj shout in a mike all night (I have nothing against that if it is your thing) but instead of doing that I heard wisdom in the quiet and cool of the night and that changes everything.

Recommended Scripture: 1 Kings 12
Question: How often do you hear and listen to a wise voice speaking?

WISE MEN DO RIGHT

"A wise man's heart is at his right hand; but a fool's heart at his left"

Ecclesiastes 10:2

Wisdom produces righteous behavior. There are two kinds of wisdom the Bible talks about earthly and heavenly wisdom. James3:17 says:

The wisdom that is from God produces the righteous traits of:

- Purity
- Peaceful
- Reasonable
- Merciful
- Consistent

Allowing us to impact the world around us as we live in right standing with God and men. The traits of a truly wise person is that they do right because they have the right things embedded in their hearts.

Recommended Scripture: James 3
Question: Do you have the earthly or heavenly wisdom?

REVERSE PSYCHOLOGY

"Folly is set in great dignity, and the rich sit in a low place. I have seen servants upon horses and princes walking as servants upon the earth."

Ecclesiastes 10:6-7

What do you do when what doesn't normally happen, happens to you? When what you thought you wanted, I would use it to let you think you wanted it because you really wanted it but only because I wanted you to have it. That's what reverse psychology does to you. I have had my fair share of it and believe me it's a real bummer. That's what I see happening here in this verse. The prince should be riding, and the servant should be walking but in a reverse psychology conversation.

The servant says to the prince "Hey prince, aren't you a bit tired of riding, don't you want to stretch those legs"

The prince says "Sure, I want to walk anyways because I see this other prince passing by walking.

Meanwhile the other prince passing by walking thinks "I sure should get back on my horse."

He hops back on and the other prince hops off his. The servant hops on the horse and then the prince starts walking. Meanwhile the other prince, let's say young Solomon (the proposed writer) sees the scene. Aha! Reverse psychology and from a kingly perspective these things ought not to be so.

Recommended Scripture: 2 Chronicles 1
Question: Why do you want what you want?

PROPHETIC DIRECTION

"If the iron be blunt, and he do not whet the edge, then must he put to more strength: but wisdom is profitable to direct"

Ecclesiastes 10:10

Wisdom carries profound prophetic effect upon environments and people. It changes, restructures and aligns things with the order of Heaven. Wisdom is the tip of prophetic edge, it gives it its cutting force because it is sharp enough to cut through lies and misdirection, it is able to shift and cut because it is born of a strong substance – the substance of grace. Wisdom is indeed profitable to direct, because one word of wisdom can give you clarity and focus to continue in the right direction for years. Is wisdom in your GPS arsenal?

Recommended Scripture: 1 Kings 20
Question: Have you ever had a word of wisdom?

SHE BIT ME

"Surely the serpent will bite without enchantment, and a babbler is no better"

Ecclesiastes 10:11

There is an old proverb that says be careful of your thoughts for they become words, be careful of your words they become action, be careful of your actions they become habits, be careful of your habits they become your life. Sometimes when we say so much because we think so much, we do the wrong thing that keeps us getting hurt by the same people we expect to protect us. But the truth is — we know better.

There is a way to know when to protect yourself in conversations with other persons. Not everyone can handle a conversation with you. Sometime ago I learnt this when I had a friend who would constantly tell me bad things about other persons in hope of receiving advice. I dismissed it as only advice-seeking and respect for my viewpoint. But in the days later it would have proven that she bit me, and she did it behind my back. Add those together and you should know what I mean. She did the same thing to me she did with other people. I got bit. Backbitten.
Just be careful in your conversations to assess whether or not someone can handle a conversation with you. It is really not about them it's about you. Next time she won't bite me.

Recommended Scripture: 2Kings 5
Question: Have you ever backbited anyone?

LACK DIRECTION

"The labor of the foolish wearieth everyone of them, because he knoweth not how to go to the city"

Ecclesiastes 10:15

Have you ever been to an unknown city? Can you imagine roaming through New York City without GPS? I tried it once and felt so confusing. I felt like I was lost, looking up into the sky I felt as if I was in a maze. The sight of my eyes were amazing but when I lifted up my eyes, I felt so small. I can't explain it. Can you imagine finding your first day to work in a city like that without GPS? It would constantly be hard. This happened to me once I went to work the first day not knowing where to go.

Fumbling and trying to find my way, I got to work late and exhausted. Most of my energy was spent walking up and down trying to find my destination. Work became harder than it should because I lacked direction. Had I known where I was going and prepared accordingly, my labor would have been less demanding, and I would have not been tired. Maybe I played the fool that day but the next day I didn't. The next day I knew where I was going.

Recommended Scripture: Isaiah 30
Question: What could have been averted if you knew where you where going?

TELL THE MATTER

"Curse not the king, no not in thy thought; and curse not the rich in thy bedchamber: for a bird of the air shall carry the voice, and that which hath wings shall tell the matter."

Ecclesiastes 10:20

Have you ever heard the saying "Your voice is in the wind?" That is because sound travels through air, solid and liquid matter. Sound is able to pass through any material and can be transmitted from one place to another. That is how both your mental and physical sound can travel. It can be carried and transmitted from one location to another. There are deeper truths about this we are yet to learn but I am sure we can be certain of this that words can travel. Both in the natural and spiritual. What are you allowing to travel?

Recommended Scripture: John 4

MULTIPLIE STREAMS OF INCOME

"Give a portion to seven, and also to eight; for thou knowest not what evil shall be upon the earth."

Ecclesiastes 11:2

What happens when you divide up a sum of money and put into different bags or baskets? Rules like the 50:30:20 and the compound interest effect teach us that overtime if you put a little away the multiplied effect will be beneficial in the long run. Conventional wisdom tells us not to put all your eggs in one basket but here heavenly wisdom is telling us something similar, divide your portion (income) into seven and eight. In other words, let your income be in seven streams where they can be distributed into each channel. This way you safeguard yourself from any potential disaster. Jacob used this truth when he went to meet his brother Esau. He perhaps had a fear of losing it all and protected himself from doing so by dividing up his portion. (see Genesis 32:7). You should do this as well. Ensure your savings, investments and income are divided and allocated well so that if one goes down, you have plenty to bank on.

Recommended Scripture: Genesis 32
Question: How many streams of income do you have?

REPLENSHING

"If the clouds be full of rain, they empty themselves upon the earth: and if the tree fall toward the south, or toward the north, in the place where the tree falleth, there it shall be."
Ecclesiastes 11:3

Nature is built to last. God in his wisdom created everything to last and replenish. He blessed the Earth and commanded this in Genesis saying:

"And God blessed them and said to them, Be fruitful, multiply, and fill the earth and subdue it [using all its vast resources in the service of God and man] and have dominion over the fish of the sea, the birds of the air and over every living creature upon the Earth."

This concept of replenishing is found all throughout the scriptures. To replenish means to be full, to fill, be accomplished or to fill the hand. Replenishing is the natural pattern God instituted for the continuation of the Earth and every living thing in it replenishes. In this verse the author tells us when the clouds are filled, they are emptied. Rain falls and when trees fall to the ground, the same place it falls, after the seeds are dispersed and germinate, that is the same place it grows again. There is something similar to this that Job speaks of:

"For there is hope of a tree, if it be cut down, that it will sprout again, and that the tender branch thereof will not cease. Though the root thereof wax old in the earth and the stock thereof die in the ground, yet through the scent of water it will bud and bring forth boughs like a plant."
Job 14:8

Job should be able to tell us about replenishing for after he had lost almost everything, it would have seemed life – his life had been cut down. But oh! Not for long, at the scent of water his replenishing came and he began to grow and bloom again. Hope is still alive friends. And it is still saying to us Hold On Pain Ends.

Recommended Scripture: Job 42
Question: Are you being replenished right now or in need of replenishing?

THE DAYS OF NO PLEASURE

Solomon encourages young people to place the creator in their memory while they are young when they have not yet encountered evil days. I didn't even know days can be evil. First nets now days, there is much we have learnt from Ecclesiastes haven't we?

These evil days he says can come near and in those times, you will say there is no more pleasure. Those are the days of no pleasure. He lists 20 characterstics of this evil day that we will look at:

- Heavenly lights darkened – sight is impaired
- The clouds of depression return after the rain of tears – You are sad even after crying
- The hands and arms tremble – lose bodily strength
- The feet and the knees bow themselves – can't move again
- The molar teeth cease because they are few – cannot eat
- Your lips are shut – don't want to walk again
- Your voice and hear is low – can't speak loud
- Afraid
- White hair blossoms – past the time of your prime
- A little thing is a burden
- Desire and appetite fail
- Silver cord of life is loosed
- Golden bowl is broken
- Poor circulation

Before all of these happen to you. Solomon is saying serve the lord.

Recommended Scripture: Ecclesiastes 12
Question: Are you in the days of pleasure?

HELP ME UP

> "For if they fall, the one will lift up his fellow: but woe to him that is alone when he falleth; for he hath not another to help him up."
>
> Ecclesiastes 4:12

Asking for help where it is needed can be a task that breaks down pride. The need to rely on and depend on someone can be a humbling experience especially for an independent adult. Not having enough strength to rise up while depending on someone to use thieves to support you, surely can teach a lesson in humility. This complex when applied in the Spirit is just as humbling as when people fall without any form of support around.

A spiritual fall is often as a result of negligence to deal with an issue or struggle. Falls can be accidental, embarrassing and sometimes injurious but the most important thing is what you do after a fall. Do you stay in that state, grope in the pain and then rise up or do you call for help, get help, heal and get moving again? It really doesn't matter how you get up. The missing element is often who helps you up and who is around when you fall. Sometimes you fall and there is no one around to help you but you can reach out to someone and reach out to God and say God I need your help, restore me, help me up again.

Maybe you are not the one that needs to pray this prayer, but maybe you need to pray this prayer for someone.

Galatians 6:1 (AMP) says:

> "Brethren, if any person is overtaken in misconduct or sin of any sort, you who are spiritual [who are responsive to and

controlled by the Spirit] should set him right and restore and
reinstate him, without any sense of superiority and with all
gentleness, keeping an attentive eye on yourself, lest you
should be tempted also."

Recommended scripture: John 17
Question: How often do you fall back into old sins or habits?

HE'S ON THE GRIND

"There is one alone, and there is not a second, yea, he hath neither child nor brother: yet is there no end of all his labor; neither is his eye satisfied with riches; neither is his eye satisfied with riches; neither saith he, For whom do I labor, and bereave my soul of good? This is also vanity, yea it is a sore travail"

Ecclesiastes 4:8

There is something good about a go getter attitude. You see, you plan, you work and execute to ultimately achieve your goal. People who have this kind of mindset can often be accused of being one track minded, stuck up or even plain and downright boring. If you are a go getter you know what it feels like. You have a motivating force.

This verse speaks of a fellow go-getter. Someone who threw off his personal pleasure to be focused on his work. But this go-getter was only that a go getter. He didn't give. He was alone and didn't stop working. He finally asked himself one day, for who am I working and why do I have no pleasure. You see my friends he was only a go getter, working and messing, working an achieving only for the sake of achieving only for the sake of amassing and achieving. Soon he had no fulfillment. He realized that he was a go-getter yes, achieved his goals, yes but in the process did not enjoy his life. Maybe he should have been both a go-getter and a go-giver and in return he would have had the fulfilment that ought to accompany the rewards of our labors. Are you a go-getter or better yet are you a go-giver?

Recommended scripture: Luke 21
Question: Are you a go-getter or a go-giver?

PAYING VOWS

"When thou vowest a vow unto God, defer not to pay it; for he hath no pleasure in fools: pay that which thou hast vowed."

Ecclesiastes 5:4

In this particular scripture it mentions the importance of paying vows before God. First and foremost, we must understand that vows are serious thing. They [vows] must not be taking lightly. Secondly, we must understand what a vow is and what is it is not . A vow is a pledge you make about something, or to someone. Vows to God can be more intricate and have more serious implications.

Let's take a look on the life of a prominent Bible character, by the name of Sampson. The Bible makes reference to his vows. According the Bible, Sampson was an Israelite who had made a covenant with God. He had made a vow from his childhood. He had taken the Nazarite vow , which led him to lead his life by strict disciplines.

Numbers 6 tells us of the Nazarite vow:

"Speak unto the children of Israel, and say unto them, When either man or woman shall separate themselves to vow a vow of a Nazarite, to separate themselves unto the Lord: He shall separate himself from wine and strong drink, and shall drink no vinegar of wine, or vinegar of strong drink, neither shall he drink any liquor of grapes, nor eat moist grapes or dried. All the days of his separation shall he eat nothing that is made of the vine tree, from the kernels even to the husk."

Numbers 6: 2-4

The vow of a Nazarite was very strict. For it required separation from many daily comforts.

It is clear from reading his story that his strict observance of this vow led him to discipline himself to be integral to his vow. However, in the latter portion of his life Sampson broke his vows and thus lost his anointing. His life displays what a covenant life with God looks like.

This covenant life is a life that had given him numerous responsibilities and obligations both to himself and his nation. Maybe you are like Sampson and have made vows. Although many people fear making vows. Vows are not dangerous. The danger is not in making a vow. Vows can be a good thing. But often it's the type of vows and whom you are making it unto. I encourage you to make a vow to God to serve him and live for him and live a covenant life loving and serving him. I am sure you will not regret it.

Recommended Scripture: Judges 16
Question: Are there any vows you need to pay?

LEADERSHIP AND CHARACTER

"If thou seest the oppression of the poor, and violent perverting of judgement and justice in a province, marvel not at the matter: for he that is higher than the highest regardeth; and there be higher than they."

Ecclesiastes 5:8

In this chapter I would like to talk about character. Of course, it's something which everyone should have, your persona and characteristics says a whole lot about you.

Firstly, what is character? It's what defines you. It's consists of your values. Character is something that will always remain one. (i.e. – it is indefinite) That's why one is called one, and two is called two. They are the same and remain the same. Your reputation is of greater value more than material things.

I would rather have a good name than to have a lot of riches. I would rather to have the right attitude and spirit, than to have friends. Leaders must protect their character. Because having a good character is very important for leadership. Remember, Jesus said by their fruits you shall know them (see Matthew 21:43). This is why it is so important because character tells the world who you are. We are living in a time where men no longer again strive to have a good character and integrity. It has become a thing of common place to be dishonest and call it 'alternative facts.'

We cannot get by for long with that kind of approach. I want you to know that character means everything, work on your character at all cost and remember that your attitude determines your altitude.

Recommended Scripture: Matthew 21

Question: Do you have a good or a bad character?

IMMERSED IN PURPOSE AND DESTINY

"For he shall not much remember the days of his life;
because God answereth him in the joy of his heart"
Ecclesiastes 5:20

True joy and passion emanate from a life that is well immersed in fulling purpose. A life that has accomplished its objectives has a deeper sense of meaning. Not everyone can truly say they have accomplished all there is to be accomplished while others can confidently say they have set targets and have met them. In this chapter I will discuss the joys of having a clearly defined purpose.

The late Dr. Myles Munroe said, "The greatest tragedy in life is not death but a life lived without it's fulfilled purpose." This is so true today. Because purpose should be the driving force behind every accomplishment in life. It should be what wakes you up in the mornings, what keeps you on the job each day. Purpose should be the engine that keeps a person who is in an awful situation when they feel like giving up. Every year there are thousands of persons - big and small , who are committing suicide. Most of these persons may have reached to a point where they felt broken. As if they have lost the true value of what life really has to offer. It is sad to think about suicide but one of the reasons why people are often driven to despair is because of a lack/lost sense of purpose.

Studies have shown over that one of the primary motivators to excel is to create action plans for our lives. Having a well define plan could be a good source of drive that will keep us going even when we don't feel like to.

When we don't feel motivated, we tend to slack up but sometimes you have to learn to motivate yourself. You must learn how to keep going even when it seems impossible for you or when the odds are up. You must learn to find that inner belief about what you truly want and the things you truly value. It is only when you are in purpose and doing what you were designed to do, that you will find true joy in your work. Life wasn't meant to be a misery with lots of disappointments . Disappointments in and of them self is not a bad thing. But it's how you use them to propels you to your destiny.

Recommended Scripture: 1 John 3 (AMP)
Question: Are you living immersed in purpose?

LIFE IS A GIFT FROM THE CREATOR

"Every man also to whom God hath given riches and wealth, and hath given him power to eat thereof, and to take his portion, and to rejoice in his labor, this is the gift of God."

Ecclesiastes 5:19

Life as we know it is a precious gift which must be protected. The gift of life is a blessing which nobody should be taking for granted . There are persons in the hospitals daily who wish they had the chance you had. Because of their health, they aren't able to life the life they desire. Life is so precious that every moment counts. It was never the creator of the universe intention for us to go through life without enjoying the most out of it. Life was meant to be lived and lived to the fullest . This is why, He has given us so many wonderful things to enjoy each day, and also given us families to share it with. If you were to share your success by yourself without anyone else, then you would be most miserable. It would rob and deprive you of the joys of having partnership success.

- What do you do when you have all that success but no one to share it with?
- How miserable and depriving would life be?

This is why when God created man, he gave him a family, so that he wouldn't be alone. To be alone with all your success is dangerous. There must be some legacy or inheritance passed down. What good would be a rich King if he had never had any successor? He would therefore be foolish.

God gave man pleasure for his soul to delight. Mismanagement of this pleasure will result in loss of life, and life is a gift. Therefore, man has to live with a caution understanding what the true meaning of enjoying life is (and what it's not.) Very often we go through life and never get the most out of it. The problem is we don't understand how to economize our life. Economize means "you try to get the most out of something." Very often people went through life without truly ever achieve anything significant. Instead of the maximum, they lived on the minimums of life. I hope this will not be your portion but that you will make the most of this precious gift of life from God.

DON'T LOSE YOUR SOUL JUST TO GAIN THE WORLD

"All the labor of man is for his mouth, and yet the appetite is not filled."

Ecclesiastes 6:7

Jesus once said what does it profit a man to gain the world and lose his own soul. (Matthew 16:26) He was stating that you could have all the world's goods that it has to offer, yet if you lack true joy and peace of mind, what profit would that be to you? If you have all the materials wealth and don't have peace and joy, you have nothing. There are many who are selling their souls. Many have sold out to things yet not to Christ. It is imperative to understand that without Christ in the vessel what truly have nothing. Because the soul could never be exchanged for anything, it could never be exchanged for vanity . The question still remains unanswered, what does it profit you? The answer is simple because there's nothing in the world to be exchanged with a man's soul. There is nothing so valuable in which one can say "Here I my soul take it" because that's how much the soul is valuable and precious.

Our soul is very expensive. Understanding your value will never lead you to the place where you will sell your soul. Today many peoples are trying to do a lot of things for hype and for fame. There are those who are selling themselves short for opportunity . But we remember how Satan once tempted Jesus on a mount. Remember he told him to fall down and worship him after he (Satan) had showed Jesus all the glories of this world in a moment of time. Jesus rebuked him.

In conclusion let us try our earnest best not to succumb to the enemy's trap. Try not to fall for the things of this world, but rather have eyes for Jesus and seek after righteousness.

Recommended Reading: Luke 11
Question: Do you understand the value of your soul?

FIGHT FOR WHAT YOU WANT

"Again, I considered all travail and every right work, that for this a man is envied of his neighbor. This is also vanity and vexation of spirit."

Ecclesiastes 4:4

We must all fight for what we want in life. Fighting for a good reason is worth more than not fighting at all. It's better to be aimed than not to be aimed at all. It's better to go for your dreams than not to sit on the sidelines hoping and go for it at all. Sometimes in life you have to fight for what you want. You have to know what you want, and then once that is clear go for it. Don't live life with the notion that if only I had known, or if only I had made my move earlier. A lot of persons are in a place where they are saying to themselves, if only I had known or tried harder, I would have made it. Very often the problem is lot of persons don't know the seriousness of an opportunity until they lose it and then they said oh!

Nothing that you will ever gain in this life will come without a fight. It will take a fight before you can gain something. Nothing in life is easy. You have to work hard for what you want. You have fight for what you want in life. The thing is we always want it to be easy we always want it to be smooth but God never promised a smooth path. There is going to be some bumps along the way. Some rough patches here and there. It can't all be easy. You have to get to a place where your mind is made up and you decide that 'Hey am going to give it my all. I am going to do whatever it takes because I have decided that this is what I want. It is interesting to know that while we may be trying to do something of value or importance, there will always be someone who is there to try to stop us.

There will always be someone who may seems not to like us or trying to sabotage us but that's when you must keep fighting along knowing that is just a matter of time before the tables are turned and you will have in your hand what you fought for. The struggle will be over. Never back down because the fight is too tough. Stand and fight. Great men and women will always be fought. Keep this in mind and keep on going.

Recommended Reading: Judges 9
Question: What am I fighting for?

THE FUTILITY OF LIFE

"For who knoweth what is good for man in this life, all the days of his vain life which he spendeth as a shadow? For who can tell a man what shall be after him under the sun?"

Ecclesiastes 6:12

When we think of the futility of life, it makes us think about all the sorrows and depravity of man. I believe that life as we know it is a gift from the creator, but man seems to not understand and appreciate this beautiful gift. We have a whole lot of people today who aren't enjoying life the way they want and conversely aren't making the most out of it.

Time is like currency – you have to make the most out of it. Everyday can be a struggle and every year things all around are getting harder. As we watch the news daily, we hear of the inflation and the rising taxes. We have bills to pay and food we must eat daily, school fees to cover and kids we have to send to school, debts to clear and a hungry world to feed. When we stop to consider it all, life can carry many miseries and worries. But the Bible states clearly, we must not worry at all. (see Matthew 6:25)

One of the keys to living is learning to trust God in everything. Learning to pray is also good. God expects us to enjoy life on his terms rather than how we may desire it to be. This is where I see a lot of people miss it. They want to live a life that is not pleasing to God, they want to acquire a success that is not biblically sound.

True success comes from knowing, believing, applying and receiving God. True success is never without God. Misery comes not when we have gained wealth, success and riches but when we aren't effective.

THE FUTILITY OF LIFE (PART II)

A lot of leaders today are very wealthy but have made little impact in reaching out to a dying world. What's the sense of having all the riches you can in the world and yet lack one thing: being effective. This is one the reasons why the world's system is crumbling today. We can see it all over.

Let's talk about the church for a bit. This is not a bash against the church (I am a believer in Christ.) But the church of the 21 century has lost its level of effectiveness. Over the past years I believe we have allowed the enemy to creep in and steal away our effectiveness. It's never about the size of our churches but rather the effect of the church on the community. I think the reason for this is because we have lost the heart and fire we once had. These days it is more about making money rather than making disciples. Persons are using church networking as a means and way of building their own selfish ambitions, rather than building the kingdom of God. I am not saying God doesn't wants us to be successful. (That's not what am saying at all but I am saying seek to populate heaven first.)

THE FUTILITY OF LIFE PART III

We have persons who may have alot of money but if it is not being useful to the kingdom of God it is demonic. As one well famous preacher says, "We have preachers who have all the riches in the world , and still don't have any power." Something is wrong with that picture. If you have that much power, then you should be able to help the sick and deliver the needy. If you are a person with that much influence what can you do to help your community.
It's never about gaining more money. It is about winning more souls and populating heaven. Thus, we have rich powerless Christian's who can't take a headache off a dog and make it bark.

Now, this not only goes for the church but for the world in general because leadership globally is affected by what occurs in the church. We are all facing challenges daily. In the midst of all the crises, what is most important should be character and this is what we must go back to developing so that we can all rise together above the futility, above the noise, above the challenges we face.

Recommended Reading: Job 29
Question: What is most important to you in life?

BUSINESS PARTNERSHIP

"Two are better than one; because they have a good reward for their labour."

Ecclesiastes 4:9

Imagine a business of which you are the chief executive officer (C.E.O). You have to manage all the administrative duties, expenses and income. Owning a business requires a lot of time and work which as the head you will need to spend a lot of time thinking about it both as the head and with your team as a collective. Business-minded individuals think in terms of a team. They work with a team who in turn help them to complete a goal. Most endeavors we partake of in life require a team. A good team will produce good success.

The same applies to friendships as well. When you have a good friend, it is a blessing. Cherish good friendships because it will yield good things. Value those who are around you who impact you positively. Those who you know are purposefully contributing good things in your life. You have to understand that not everyone comes in our life with a purposefully, some enter for other reasons. Having a good confidant will help you to become who you are supposed to be. There should be a mutual bond between you and your confidant, where you benefit them, and they also benefit you. However, very often we find that there are many who just want what they can get, rather than what they can do to help a person. Sometimes people's lives are in shambles and all they need is a little help or push to start. When the right connection comes along, their life will become more productive.

You need people who are there for you to support you along the way, peoples who are for what you are for. Because not everyone is for you and for what you support. Many hang around for selfish ambitions , and for what they can take. If you have two or three confidants, I consider you to be a blessed person. Good friendships are good partnerships, in the long run they will bless your life enormously.

Recommended Reading: Joshua 8
Question: Do you have a confidant?

BUSINESS PARTNERSHIPS PART II

It is imperative to have a friend, a partner, a companion because along the way you are going to need people. Never think for a second that you won't need help. No man is an island and no man can stand alone. There are times when you will need someone who can support you, who can encourage, who can help you up out of a situation. Your going to need someone who might be better off and in the right position to support.

Let's think about this statement for a second : "Two is better than one." This statement shows us that if we are to make it, we must invest in others. We must value true friendships and seek to build firm relationships so that in the long run we are benefited. Being selfish, arrogant and not a people person will not carry us far in life because if you are rich and get to the top alone, while standing on the top you will realize how much alone you are. You look left and then you look right but you will see no one there with you. How happy would that be? You wouldn't feel happy enough to enjoy all your successes. The price paid for success would then amount to the price of misery. These things should not be.

If all of the pleasures of success could not be enjoyed or shared, why bother? If all the persons along the way who had supported you, who were there for you, toiled with you had not. You would realize that if it hadn't been for those few key persons, you wouldn't be where you are now. Because those precious people were there to help curve and steer you, to help pave and cut the path for your feet to trod. They were there to help build the project from the start. And so, you would clearly see that people do play a major role in our lives. There is a good reward in laboring together.

Don't be too caught up with your own ambitions and personal success so much that you forget about unity. Don't just focus on you only. Focus also on the community around you. Your community is your power, it's your life . The idea here is to "invest in good friendships and relationships that are worthwhile." Don't waste your time where you'll lose it but instead invest it and you will reap the rewards.

Recommended Reading: Ruth 4
Question: Who are your key partners in life?

CONCEPTS OF TIME

"To everything there is a season, and a time to every purpose under the heaven."

Ecclesiastes 3:1

Proper timing is everything. When we think about time, we often think of it in "moments" and "measures." But I want you to see time as a measure or a spec of eternity. The Greeks use different words for time. One such word is "Kairos." Kairos is that opportune moment or appointed time.

This is where we get the concept of Kairos time. Kairos is that opportune time when whatever we attempt will happen. It is your moment in time to shine. Sometimes you may want to do something or feel compelled to do it but nothing will never happen until the time is right to do so. This is a universal law. Time is inevitable - it will happen with you or without you . You have to understand that nothing you do will be able to time's continuation. Whatever you do, even if you succeeded in blowing up the moon or Sun, time would continue.

The proper thing to do with our time is learning how to manage it. The Bible says there is a time and a place for all things. It is important for us to understand the fact that if we want the right results in life, we have to be able to properly manage our time. Let's look at proper time management in a work context. At your workplace you are given 8 hours daily to complete a shift while you are also required to report to work at an expected time. If you are late without any explanation and report to work, they will reprimand you. In the workplace there is a way how you must conduct yourself. How you behave well will determine how far you will reach in the company.

Sometimes you may not like how they treat you or how you have been treated but you must always maintain a level of professionalism. I am saying this to show you that your attitude will always determine your altitude.

Sometimes there will be times when you may want to confront but you cannot. You may want to judge certain things, but you cannot until the perfect (opportune) time. In matters of judgement, decorum, tactfulness and proper timing is not only good, but it is crucial. There is truly a time for every matter. There is a time to judge a situation and then there is a time to keep quiet. You will not always need say or act. The key is to know when to say or to act.

There are different concepts of time. Both the Hebrews and Greeks had their own concepts. "Kairos" and "Chronos" time is Greek, while other concepts like "Et" and "yum" are Hebrew. The Bible mentions the sons of Issachar who had an understanding of the times and seasons. Having an understanding of the timing and seasons will cause us to not make wrong decision in life. Therefore, a proper understanding of timing leads to proper planning. Having a clear plan for our lives will help to eliminate wrong choices, as well as help us to properly manage our time. As you grow older you will understand that you can't waste any more time. We can't handle our time loosely. Thus, effective management of time will help us to best utilize it to release our potential.

It's was Dr. Myles Munroe who once said, "The greatest tragedy in life is not death, but what's dies on the inside." Therefore, effective living is not necessarily a matter of length, or how long you lived, but rather the quality of your life.

There are many people who have lived for years without ever been effective. They lived a menial life without ever impacting the world. The purpose of effective living is living a life where you have impacted the world by living a life that bring glory to God. All of us are here on Earth for a reason, and that reason is in God. Our #1 priority should be knowing what is God's will for our life is and doing it. The will of God should be your life's blueprint. When we do know what it is, it will sort of steer and guide us in the path of success.

Recommended Reading: Deuteronomy 16
Question: Do you manage your time wisely?

POTENTIAL

"Whatsoever thy hand findeth to do, do it with thy might; for there is no work, nor device, nor knowledge, nor wisdom, in the grave, wither thou goest."

Ecclesiastes 9:10

When we think of the word potential we often think of our own strengths, abilities and gifts. Everyone has potential on the inside of them. God has created all of us with potential. Potential is one of the things that makes us unique as individuals. Although everyone has it, everyone has a special amount of potential to be something great, to be the person who God wants them to be.

It is my joy each and every day to release my true greatness. I often imagine the great things I can do for God through his Holy Spirit. Greatness is what we were all made for. The Bible declares that man was created in the image and the likeness of God. We were created in the image and likeness of our Creator, who is the greatest of the greatest.

To release this greatness, I have to begin to use up all the gifts, talents and abilities God has placed in me. Utilizing your skill is key. If we are to be very effective in this world, we have to make ourselves useful to it. Being useful to our society is a primary goal we must achieve. I believe the key to living successfully, effectively and efficiently is to discover your own authentic creativity.

In this verse, the ecclesiastical writer was saying we must do whatever our hands find best to do. In other words, get busy, we must not waste any more time in life. Our live span is really short and so we must learn to manage our time. If we are to be effective in delivering our services to the world, our time has to be managed well.

Once we understand that life is short then we will understand the urgency pertaining to the matters of our destiny and thereby see it fit to release our maximum potential. All of us have been placed here on Earth to fulfill a great purpose and that purpose will not be fulfilled unless we release our true potential. We will find the joy and passion that comes with life as we do this.

There is a beauty and a joy that come when we discover and find our purpose. Life was meant to be lived and lived to the fullest extent. The sky is our limit thus we must aim for the sky. Purpose is the sole essence of our existence on Earth. Sometimes to discover purpose, we have to search for it. By searching I mean to learn to see a need and fill that need. In order to be effective, we have to first assess our own potential and then work towards releasing it. Finding a need could be a best place to start. The text says anything that we find to do in life we are to do with the best of our ability. Do that thing with your might and power. Do it in a way that nobody could ever do it better. The late Martin Luther King Jr once said "sweep streets like Michelangelo would make art." Therefore, Dr. King was saying we are to do it to the best of our ability, give it our all. If you are going to do something in life, do it with a difference. Do it so that the world would come one day and say here lived a genius. It's time to start sweep streets with the best of our ability. Do it with your might. When we give it our might we are sure to obtain a more rewarding result. The next thing is we cannot carry anything with us to the grave, we must leave it all behind. The late Dr Myles Munroe once said, "The cemetery is the wealthiest place on Earth." Because when we don't take time to release our potential and empty ourselves before we die, we go the grave full and that is a travesty. A travesty that you should not let happen to you or your grave.

Recommended Reading: 2 Sammuel 12:11
Question: Have you released your God-given potential?

THE EMPTINESS OF MEN'S SOUL

The whole pursuit of man in life is to find satisfaction for his own soul. His whole pursuits, inherent desires, cravings is to find something that he thinks can truly makes him happy. Indeed, there is an inherent need, a deep void in the vastness of his soul. Such desires are ones which he alone cannot truly fulfill. There is only one thing and one thing alone that his soul needs.

First and foremost, it is imperative to know that he [man] had lost a kingdom. Secondly, he [man] lost the most important thing which is his relationship with God. Ever since the garden of Eden, man's soul had been ravished badly, his soul had become destitute void of glory. What he had lost was that thing which could satisfy his soul.
This is why we find many around the world who are empty, lost, miserable and without a sense of purpose. They may try everything they could and yet still they feel empty. There soul is void of glory, there life is empty. The reason is because man have lost God who can truly fill his life. He has lost his prime thing in life which to have a relationship with the Holy Spirit .

Recommended Reading: Ezekiel 10
Question: Is your life devoid of Glory?

THE SORROWS OF THE RICH

"A man to whom God hath given riches, wealth and honor, so that he wanteth nothing for his soul of all he desireth, yet God giveth him not power to eat thereof, but a stranger eatheth it: this is vanity, and it is an evil disease."

Ecclesiates 6:2

A very interesting paradox that exists within the modern world is what I would term the powerlessness of the rich. Yes, as I observe it and you observe it. We all know that the rich only gets richer and the poor only gets poorer. The rich keeps on gaining more and more and there seems to be no ending to their gaining. The problem is not with their gain but how make a difference through their riches. In today's world we have a lot of peoples who are wealthy but they are not effective. We see this not only among the rich but in every aspect of modern life. For example, in church with leaders. There are many who have a whole lot of riches and still ain't got no power. Drive nice cars and still ain't got no power.

When the Bible talks about the dangers of riches, God is not talking about not having money.

Let's take a look at 1 Timothy 6:9-10:

"But they that will be rich fall into temptation and a snare and into many foolish and hurtful lusts, which drown men in destruction and perdition. For the love of money is the root of all evil: which some coveted after, they have erred from the faith, and pierced themselves through with many sorrows."

The writer of the text is not talking about not valuing monetary gains but rather he is talking about loving it to the point where you forget about God. The verse speaks of sorrows which accompany this which makes reference to letting riches control your life to the point where God is no longer first preference and first place. Godly sorrow is good but ungodly sorrow is bad. The Bible states the blessings of the Lord makes rich and he adds no sorrows unto it. (see Proverbs 10:22) No sorrows will be added God says when he blesses.
It also says sorrows will be multiplied when one chases after another God. Of course, there is only one true and living God. There is only one. Therefore, riches become evil unto us when we let it take first preference rather than the Lord.

> Trust not in oppression, and become not vain in robbery: if riches increase set not your heart upon them.
>
> Psalm 62:10

In conclusion riches are good for a worthy cause to help someone but the sorrows are to the wicked who does not serve God.

Recommended Reading: Luke 16
Question: Am I a charitable person?

AVOIDING THE EVIL OF NOT BEEN EFFECTIVE

"There is an evil which I have seen under the sun, and it is common among men:"

Ecclesiastes 6:1

One of the dangerous things that can happen with us is when we reach the place where we lose our influence and impact. Many want the power, the fame, popularity, the wealth and status, but thou all of that may seem great, if we are not reaching those who are to be reached then we are useless. There is nothing terrible as been useless . We were all born to make impact on this world. We are all unique and have our own unique style of impacting our world. The world today needs those who will impact and make a difference in this 21 century.

There are many billionaires and millionaires in today's world, but what are they doing to make this planet a peaceful and better place? How are they reaching the sick, the homeless, the orphaned, those who are victims to trafficking and the list goes on?

Today, I want you reflect and consider the fact that it is not about how you lived or how long you lived but rather how effective where you in reaching others. What legacy will you leave behind and what impact you had made to the world?

Recommended Reading: 1 Corinthians 16:9
Question: What do you want to be remembered for?

KEEP HIM BUSY

"For he shall not remember the days of his life; because God answereth him in the joy of his heart."

Ecclesiastes 5:19

Joy comes from discovering and executing that purpose and passion you have. In this chapter, we will focus on the fact that God really wants to grant man his desires. It may be hard for you to believe but indeed He does. Have you ever laid out a plan before and then allowed that plan to just consume all of your time? I would imagine you will be fully immersed in these goals, so much so to the point your time becomes scarce.

This is what the creator does. He actually keeps us busy with the things in his heart. He does grant our desire, which is what the verse is saying. The question should not be a matter if he's going to grant it because he will. It is therefore important for us to understand that only desires that are inline will his will and counsel he will grant. He gives us the desires of the heart only for a purpose. This is what the verse is saying that the purpose of these kinds of answered prayers is to keep you busy. It seems to me God does not want us to be idle and to be a busy body but to be fully cooperative in stewarding what he gives us.

Being busy is good but it is what keeps you busy. It is what occupies your own space and time.

Recommended Reading: Matthew 20:8
Question: Do I understand the purpose of answered prayer?

THE OPPRESSION OF THE POOR

"So I returned, and considered all the oppressions that are
done under the sun: and behold the tears of such as were
oppressed, and they had no comforter; and on the side of
their oppressors there was power; but they had no
comforter."

Ecclesiastes 4:1

When we think about the injustice that is in the world it is an
uncomfortable and painful to think about. Such injustice is unhuman
to bear. No one should not have to bare its brunt. In today's world in
regions like the Middle East there are areas ravaged with war. In
places like these across the world there is no sign of peace, no love
and respect for the lives of each other. If we were to take a look at
war zones alone to consider the isolation, pain and oppression of
these downtrodden people groups, we would have to painfully think
our way through to the consensus that not only is the world unfair
but it can be a lonely place if you don't have any support.

Although we have often turned a blind eye to it, there are serious
levels of oppression going on and an such that is inhuman. Much of
the oppression and injustice is permitted by those in government
while the poor man is been oppressed every day. In Jamaica, when it
comes to government taxes and bills, they can be quite expensive.
You are stressed out with paying bills till you die. This has been my
plight as a working-class Jamaican man.

The governments are spending monetary funds on them self while
the families of the poor class man suffer poverty. The rich are
favored and held in high esteem as they give to the poor man the
whip of poverty.

Because of corruption in the government system, the rich give justice but the poor are being punished all as they strip his rights away from him. This is a real injustice and it is real to me because I see it and I feel it. But I remind myself that the Bible says that God hears the voice of the poor when they cry unto him. (see Psalm 34:6) I know and believe this oppression can and will end someday.

Recommended Reading: Psalm 34
Question: What is your stance on the injustices in your nation?

MYSTERY OF GOD, ITS INEXPRESSIBLE

"All things are full of labor; man cannot utter it: the eye is not satisfied with seeing, nor the ear filled with hearing."

Ecclesiastes 1:8

The book of Acts told us that God knows all his work that he would do from the beginning. (Acts 15:18) In Isaiah he says that God declares the end from the beginning. There we see that God knows all things from creation time.

It's is mystery. A wonderful mystery. When we think of life, we understand that it too is a mystery. We can't understand the reason why some stuff had to happen. In Job it says that his ways are past finding out. Which means that there is no way you are going to figure out the things of God. They are given to us means of divine revelation.

Only God knows the end of everything. We are just in the middle and do not see the complete picture. Always know that God is in control and is totally sovereign. God's mystery had been concealed through the ages, but he chooses those to whom he wishes to reveal his truth unto. All of life is in his mystery, but who can unravel it?

Recommended Reading: Ephesians 3
Question: What mysteries am I trying to figure out?

A GOOD PURPOSE TO THINGS

"Lo, this only have I found, that God hath made man upright; but they have sought out many inventions"

Ecclesiastes 7:29

Everything you see in life has a purpose assigned to it. Absolutely everything. Purpose is like the nucleus, a driving force of sorts. We must understand that there is a good (right, useful, beneficial) purpose for things and a bad (evil, crooked, harmful) purpose that also exists. Therefore, you have to know which purpose is at work in a given situation.

Let us think for a second about a car. A car's purpose is clearly for driving. Nobody would buy a car and then put in into a pool to drive nor would one takes it and place it into a refrigerator. That is just not the purpose. Let's look at another example. Let's say the internet, you can use it for good purposes and bad. One can use it to access valuable information as well as to scam or hack. At the end of the day it's a matter of what you use a particular thing for.

Recommended Reading: Acts 11
Question: Am I using things for the purpose they were created?

POWER OF INVESTING

"In the morning sow thy seed, and in the evening withhold
not thine hand: for thou knowest withhold not thine hand:
for thou knowest not whether shall prosper, either this or
that or whether they both shall be alike good."

Ecclesiastes 11:6

Diligence when combined with the power of investing is
tremendous. The Bible states when we are diligently seek Him, we
will be rewarded. Diligence involves work, effort and discipline.
There are many who want blessings but don't want to work. It is a
scriptural promise that God rewards diligence. You have to be
diligent.

In life, I encourage you to never forget to invest in what you have.
Sometimes we dismiss investing and instead have a consumer
mentality but a wise person will learn and understand that whatever
you investing will eventually be what you will be rewarded, whatever
you sow you will eventually reap and with it a harvest will come.
The thing most of us lack is the disciplines to life. (If I am not
speaking for you, I will speak for myself) Most of us are lazy enough
that we no longer mind been uncomfortable. As long as it doesn't
cost us or remove us out of our comfort spots. People like this don't
like change and are resistant to it. Discipline rids us this condition.
When we become more disciplined at life it will make our lives better.
Not only will you reap the harvest of multiplied and consistent effort,
but you will also reap a track record of excellence as you grow and
harness the power of diligence.

Recommended Reading: Jeremiah 17
Question: Are you a diligent person?

JOYS OF MARRIAGE

"Live joyfully with the wife whom thou lovest all the days of the life of thy vanity, which he hath given thee under the sun, all the days of thy vanity: for that is thy portion in this life, and in thy labour which thou takest under the sun."

Ecclesiastes 9:9

Investing in your relationships should be a top-priority for you. Nothing tells more about a person than the depth and quality of their relationships. At end of your life it's what u have left, money will not stand beside your casket, food, clothes and shelter wont either, it will be the people who you did life with.

An important relationship some people will embark on is marriage. Of a truth marriage is a very sacred thing. There is nothing like when two people of the opposite sex come together as one. It was never God's intention for a man to be alone. That is why he created the woman for the man.

In today's society, we are seeing a whole bunch of people who are making the decision to be married. Marriage is honorable and the bed is undefiled. It is beautiful to look at because it represents harmony and unity. However, this unit can quickly turn from sweet to sour if not guided by the principles of God's Word. God intended for our family to be at peace. He loves unity and togetherness. We have to learn how to invest in our marriage life by learning to cultivate it and make it even better.

Neither the male nor the female is perfect, but God has commanded us that husband's should love his wives as Christ loves the church and also gave himself for it and wives too should also love their husbands dearly.

Recommended Reading: Ephesians 5
Question: What makes up a happy marriage for you?

CORRECT TIMING

"I returned, and saw under the sun, that the race is not to the swift, nor the battle to the strong, neither yet bread to the wise, nor yet riches to men of understand, nor yet favour to men of skill; but time and chance happened to them all."

Ecclesiastes 9:11

It is never a matter of our own abilities and strengths. It is never a matter of our intellect and our own gifts. It is about correct timing. Knowing correct timing to things is key. When we understand proper timing, we will understand and know our time. Everything has a correct timing to it. There is a time and place for everything.

Everything has with it a season for every purpose under the heavens. Sometimes because we don't know timing, we often make mistakes which often could be avoidable if we proceeded carefully and made wise decisions factoring in timing. This past year I had applied for the JDF (Jamaica Defense Force) where I had passed all the entry exams and medical, but I failed the last medical and was disqualified. Having seen my friends went through which was really a big joy for me yet I still didn't understand why I couldn't make it through as well. After making it that far in the process, I still couldn't see how or why I had failed. But it wasn't after I had read in Ecclesiastes that I understood why.

Now I understand why I didn't make it. Time and chance happen to everyone. This little statement here shook me. As simple as it is, I had to ask myself this question: Is there a difference between time for me and time for you?

CORRECT TIMING PART II

The answer is simple yes there is. I have learned now that our time is all not the same. The reason it worked for them wasn't because they were any better, skillful, or stronger. It was simply because time and chance happened. Yes, it happened to them all. It will happen with you or without you. You can't stop time. Whenever God says it is your time. It is your time and nobody can do anything about it. All we can do is to make ourselves ready for whatever opportunity lies ahead of us. I realize that it wasn't because I didn't meet all the requirements why I didn't get through with the army. It just wasn't my time and my chance. There are many people today going through similar situations where it's seems to not work towards their favor. The moment you understand that fact the better it is for you because you won't have to beat down yourself. You won't have to worry about it, all you have to do it pray about it.

That is why the Bible says in Phillipians 4:4 (MSG)

> "Don't fret or worry. Instead of worrying, pray. Let petitions and praises shape your worries into prayers, letting God know your concerns. Before you know it, a sense of God's wholeness, everything coming together for good, will come and settle you down. It's wonderful what happens when Christ displaces worry at the center of your life."

When your time comes it will be so perfect for you. Then and there you know this is what I have been waiting for, it will be your opportune moment.

Recommended Reading: Philippians 4
Question: Has time and chance ever happened to you?

THE SIN OF GREED

"He that loveth silver shall not be satisfied with silver; nor he that loveth abundance with increase: this is also vanity."

Ecclesiastes 5:10

Greediness leads to murder for persons will murder for what they want in life. One of the major problems we are facing today in the world has to be greediness. Political greediness is a plague in the 21 century. The world is not balance as it should be, and the reason is many are simply too greedy for gain. As a people we have reached to a point now where we no longer have a hand to give. We are mean and stingy. Everyone wants more but no one wants to lose it. No one wants to give and take in life anymore just take, take, take and no giving.

A greedy person doesn't care about anyone but themselves . It is a spirit that is plaguing our generation. My encouragement is let us learn how to give and how to take.

Recommended Reading: Proverbs 1:10-19
Question: Am I a giver or a taker?

SUBMIT TO THE SYSTEM

"Whoso keepeth the commandment shall feel no evil thing:
and a wise man's heart discerneth both time and judgement."
Ecclesiastes 8:5

In this chapter I want to speak about Daniel. Daniel was in Babylon and was among the captives to Babylon. By God's grace, Daniel was an elevated and was a statesman who was well favored by the king. His wisdom and attitude set him apart from among the rest. One thing about him was that he had a radical faith in Jehovah. He was very devoted and feared God. He was a praying man, and feared God. Daniel understood the kingdom, he understood the principles of it and because favor was on him, it set him apart from the rest. Daniel was also very disciplined and practical. Using Daniel as an example I encourage you to emulate his character traits.

- The right kind of attitude
- The right spirit for excellence and prosperity.
- Understanding of kingdom protocols
- And Obedience at all costs

Recommended Reading: Daniel 3
Question: Am I willing to be obedient to God no matter the cost?

THE SOVEREIGN PLAN

"He hath made everything beautiful in his time: also he hath set the world in their heart, so that no man can find out the work that God maketh from the beginning to the end."

Ecclesiastes 3:11

Discovering the will of God is very important. Learning from all setbacks, disappointments and failures is for a reason. When we Understand that nothing just happens and that you may be delayed but not denied we can exclaim "It is all apart of the script and I can be confident that all things work together for my good (Romans 8:28)

I have seen this in my own life time and time again. God has had a plan for my life and his hand has been in the making of it. The many experiences I have had of deliverance, provision and protection have showed me it's just a matter of time before the Lord shows up and puts in his hand in the matter. When we submit to God's will we quickly discover that many times it is not about if God will do his will, or promises it is often when he will do it. This is the other side to the mystery of God's will, His divine timing.

The text states that "He has made all things beautiful in its own time." It is made perfected in its own season. No matter how you may want to rush time or try to get ahead too early. Yet he has made it beautiful in its own time, the right time. The writer was saying he has already made all things beautiful in its own time. That means when the right time is come, then will everything be right that must be right. In this way we learn to trust God and see that the right time will produce right results and right results will result in the right things.

All things have a time to be perfected – a maturation date. It has its own beautiful time assigned by the Almighty God. The sovereignty of God controls all things and therefore he controls all things. All times and all seasons. Absolutely everything. He determines all that comes out of life. He knows the end from the beginning. To say he made all things beautiful in its time is to say he made all things in its own time perfect. We just get to sit back and watch the journey unfold.

Recommended Reading: Amos 7
Question: Are you enjoying your maturation process?

KEEP ON REFLECTING.

ABOUT THE AUTHORS

JEROME WRIGHT is a cook, reading-enthuiast and rising evangelical voice. He is also a Portmore resident, who enjoys watching movies, socializing and cooking. He is a past student of the Waterford Comprehensive High and the PHEART-Trust NTA. Raised in a challenging background, Jerome has had to overcome many obstacles to keep moving. He attributes his life purpose to "comforting, evangelizing, befriending and discipling." He has chosen to coauthor with Kevan Ferguson his longtime ministry associate on his first writing project, Ecclesiastical Reflections.

KEVAN FERGUSON is an author, poet and intercessor. He is the author of 7 titles which include the Laws of Spiritual Momentum, Memories in the Rain and Campus Revival. Kevan is often known for his calm disposition, encouragement and evangelical fervor. He is a former student of the University of the West Indies and is a rising prophetic voice to his region and nation.